How does a trumpet work?

Jim Pipe

Aladdin/Watts

London • Sydney

What are sounds?

Zack, Steve and Amy are helping Jo to fly her kite. "The wind is strong," says Zack, "I can hear it rushing through the trees". As the kite lifts up into the air, it flaps and buzzes noisily.

Why does your kite make that sound?

I think the wind makes it flap like a bee's wings. It makes a buzzing sound.

Let's see how the children find out.

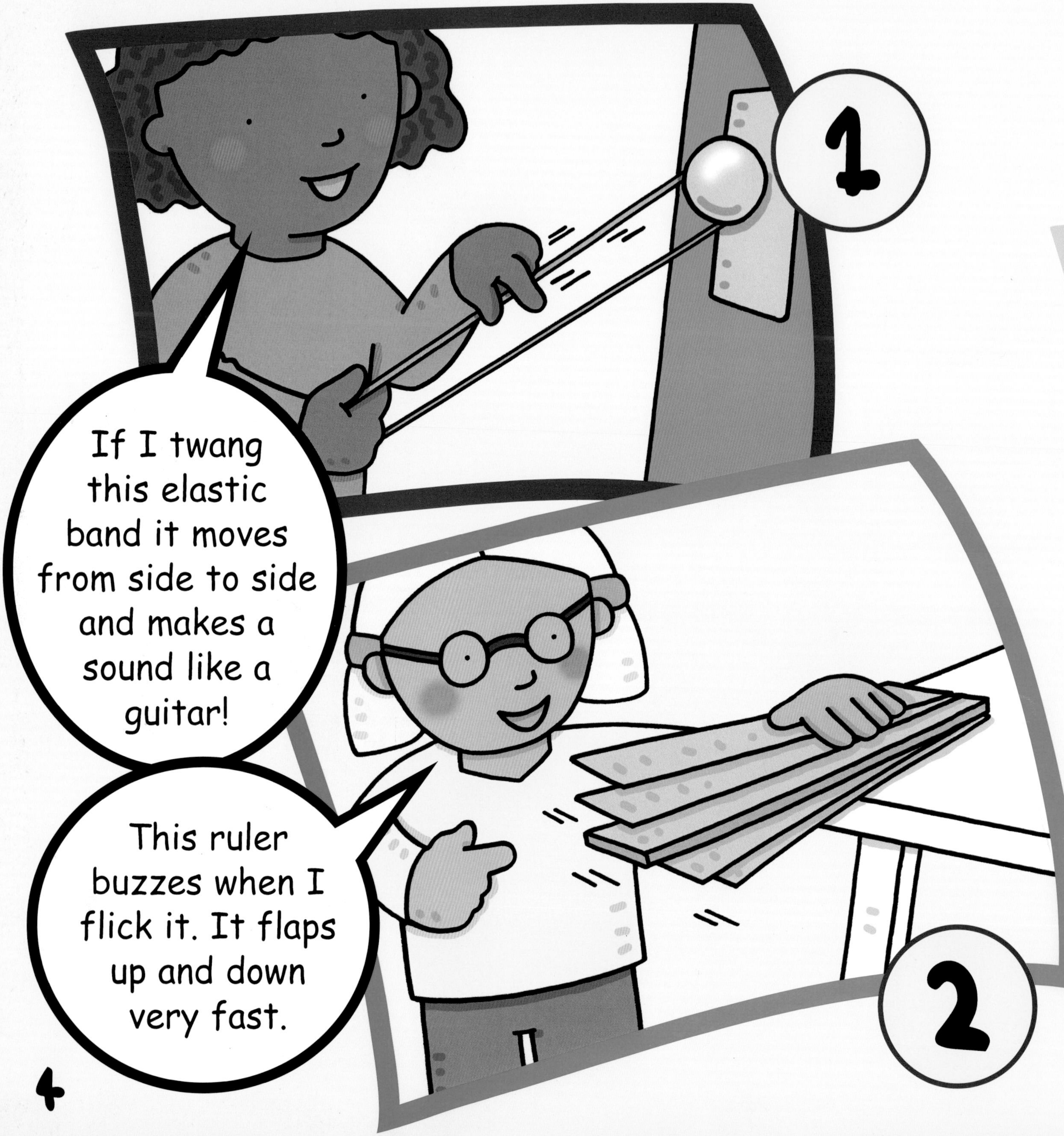

Why it works

Every sound is made by something moving backwards and forwards very quickly. When something does this, we say it vibrates. When we twang an elastic band or fly a kite, we can see and hear these movements, called vibrations. Some vibrations, however, are too small to see. But they still make a noise.

Solve the puzzle!

What vibrates or moves when you speak? Put your fingertips to your throat and talk. Can you feel anything?

Can you feel sounds?

The children walk back from the park with Zack's dad. On the way home, a car passes them in the street. It is playing very loud music. Thump! Thump! Thump!

It's so loud I can feel it!

The music in that car is very loud.

Let's see how the children find out.

3

Not too loud!

Look at the rice dance up and down! The sound of the music must make the drum vibrate.

When something makes a noise, it vibrates. It also makes the air around it vibrate. These vibrations in the air are called sound waves. They spread out in all directions like ripples on a pond. When sound waves hit something else they can make it vibrate, too. So even though you can't see sound waves, you can sometimes feel them.

Solve the puzzle

Can you feel other sounds? Blow up a balloon and tie the end. Hold the balloon close to your lips and speak. What do you feel?

9

Why do rabbits have big ears?

The children are playing with Zack's rabbit out in the garden. When a dog barks in the distance, the rabbit stops and turns its head to listen.

Look how big your rabbit's ears are!

I think big ears help a rabbit to hear well.

When something makes a noise, the sound travels through the air to your ears. The part of an ear that hears sounds is inside your head. But flaps on the outside of an ear help to direct sound into it. That's why large ears can help animals to hear better. It's also why you hear more when you cup your hand behind your ear.

Solve the puzzle

What makes sounds less noisy? Set off the alarm on an alarm clock. Then cover your ears. What happens to the sound?

13

What are echoes?

Later, the children go to the swimming pool with their friend Sam. Steve whizzes down the water slide. He lets out a loud shout and the sound echoes around the pool.

14

Let's see how the children find out.

16

Now let's try with a piece of shiny card.

3

Now I can hear the clock ticking!

So sounds bounce off hard surfaces. Echoes are sounds bouncing off the walls.

Why it works

Sounds bounce off hard, smooth surfaces, but not soft ones. If you shout in an empty hall or tunnel, you can hear a noise after you have stopped shouting. This is the sound of your voice bouncing back off the walls – an echo.

Solve the puzzle

Do sounds travel in water? Next time you have a bath (and an adult is there), lie on your back, keep your mouth and nose above the water, but let your ears go under the water. What can you hear?

17

How do trumpets and tubas work?

The children watch a marching band in the parade. There are lots of instruments. Some play high notes and some play low notes.

19

20

It has an even higher sound now. So a smaller tube of air makes a higher note.

A tuba has a big tube of air inside it. That's why it makes such a low sound when you blow into it.

3

Why it works

Each bottle contains a tube of air. When you blow across the top, the air inside vibrates. This makes a sound. Longer tubes of air make lower sounds. Shorter tubes make high sounds. So a big tuba can make very low sounds and a trumpet can make high sounds.

Solve the puzzle

Can you make an elastic band play different notes? Put it round a door handle, pull it gently and twang it. Then pull it harder and twang it again. What happens to the sound?

21

Did you solve the puzzles?

What vibrates or moves when you speak?

When you talk, you can feel your throat vibrate with your fingertips, like Steve felt the balloon vibrate on page 5. A part of your throat, called your vocal cords, moves as you speak. This makes the air in your throat and mouth vibrate. The vibrating air makes a sound which you change by moving your lips and tongue.

Can you feel some other sounds?

When you speak into the balloon it makes it vibrate and you can feel it moving. Do you remember how the CD player made the rice grains jump on page 9? Hold a balloon near a CD player, then play some music. You will feel the sound waves making the balloon vibrate.

What makes sounds less noisy?

Putting your hands over your ears stops sound from getting in, so the alarm clock seems quieter. You can also make the alarm quieter by packing it in a box with balls of scrunched up paper. They stop the sound waves from getting out.

Do sounds travel in water?

Yes! With your ears under the water you can hear low sounds easily. Sound travels through walls and other solid objects as well. Put your ear to a desk and tap it. How loud does it sound?

Can you play different notes with an elastic band?

Pulling an elastic band harder makes the sound higher. But letting it go loose again makes the sound lower. If you know someone with a guitar, ask to see how the sound of the strings can be changed by making them tight or loose.

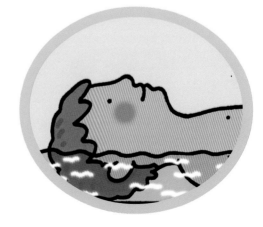

23

Index

© Aladdin Books Ltd 2002

Designed and produced by
Aladdin Books Ltd
28 Percy Street
London W1T 2BZ

First published in
Great Britain in 2002 by
Franklin Watts
96 Leonard Street
London EC2A 4XD

ISBN 0 7496 4743 4

A catalogue record for this book is
available from the British Library.

Printed in U.A.E.
All rights reserved

Literacy Consultant
Jackie Holderness
Westminster Institute of Education
Oxford Brookes University

Science Consultants
David Coates and Helen Wilson
Westminster Institute of Education
Oxford Brookes University

Science Tester
Alex Laar

Design
Flick, Book Design and Graphics

Illustration
Jo Moore